Swimming in a School

by Thea Feldman
illustrated by Luciana Navarro Alves

Scott Foresman
is an imprint of

PEARSON

Glenview, Illinois • Boston, Massachusetts • Chandler, Arizona
Upper Saddle River, New Jersey

Every effort has been made to secure permission and provide appropriate credit for photographic material. The publisher deeply regrets any omission and pledges to correct errors called to its attention in subsequent editions.

Unless otherwise acknowledged, all photographs are the property of Pearson.

Illustrations by Luciana Navarro Alves

16 ©Royalty-Free/Corbis

ISBN 13: 978-0-328-51428-1
ISBN 10:   0-328-51428-4

Copyright © by Pearson Education, Inc., or its affiliates. All rights reserved.
Printed in the United States of America. This publication is protected by copyright, and permission should be obtained from the publisher prior to any prohibited reproduction, storage in a retrieval system, or transmission in any form or by any means, electronic, mechanical, photocopying, recording, or likewise. For information regarding permissions, write to Pearson Curriculum Rights & Permissions, One Lake Street, Upper Saddle River, New Jersey 07458.

Pearson® is a trademark, in the U.S. and/or in other countries, of Pearson plc or its affiliates.

Scott Foresman® is a trademark, in the U.S. and/or in other countries, of Pearson Education, Inc., or its affiliates.

3 4 5 6 7 8 9 10   V0N4   13 12 11 10

"This school is no fun!" Leo told his friend Gil. "Every day is the same. We swim from here to there. What's the goal of this journey?"

Gil looked sad. "Oh Leo," he said. "Trust me. Swimming in a school is cool. One day you'll see why."

But Leo was staring at something far away.

"Wow!" he said. "Gil, do you see that? It looks like an old ship. What's that shiny stuff? I'll bet there could be crystal and maybe even jewels. I'm going to make a discovery!"

"Leo!" Gil said. "Don't you dare go over there. That shiny light could be one of those ugly anglerfish. It could be just waiting to eat you!"

But Gil was talking to air bubbles. Leo had already disappeared toward the ship.

Leo was very excited when he swam into the ship. Finally! Here was something different. The ship was filled with things he had never seen before.

There were big bright jewels and shiny gold coins. Leo swam toward a bright light. There he found an anglerfish with its jaws open wide!

Leo swam backwards as fast as he could. He kept his eyes on the anglerfish at all times. "Ouch!" Leo cried as he backed up right into a silver fork. "This is not the kind of adventure I wanted!"

As Leo turned around, he saw a big moray eel lurking in the corner.

"Say, son, why don't you come and tell old Morey all about it? Before I eat you, that is!"

Leo watched Morey come toward him. He knew it was time to leave.

"I must go! I must get back to the school. Maybe we can talk some other time."

As he swam away, Leo was unaware that a big net had come down. Like a giant scoop, it caught him up.

But Leo swam right through a hole in the net. For once, being small was a good thing.

Leo swam behind some coral. He needed to be safe. He needed a quiet place where he could think. He thought about his safe school. How he missed it now!

Leo looked out at the ocean. More than anything, he wanted to see Gil and the school. But what was that? The school was coming back! Leo was joyful.

"I'll never complain about swimming from here to there ever again!"

Schooling Fish

At least one-fourth of all fish swim in schools. Some schools have millions of fish! By swimming together, fish make it harder for bigger fish to eat them. Some scientists also think it's easier to find a mate in a school. Also, small fish are born knowing to swim together. It's the best defense against a sea world filled with big, hungry creatures.